Richard Rome Bealey

Field Flowers and City Chimes

Poems

Richard Rome Bealey

Field Flowers and City Chimes
Poems

ISBN/EAN: 9783337111786

Printed in Europe, USA, Canada, Australia, Japan

Cover: Foto ©ninafisch / pixelio.de

More available books at **www.hansebooks.com**

Field Flowers and City Chimes.

POEMS

BY

R. R. BEALEY,

AUTHOR OF "AFTER-BUSINESS JOTTINGS."

ILLUSTRATED BY AUGUSTUS DULCKEN.

LONDON: SIMPKIN & MARSHALL.
MANCHESTER: JOHN HEYWOOD, 143 DEANSGATE.
1866.

TO

CHARLES SWAIN, ESQ.,

𝕿𝖍𝖎𝖘 𝖁𝖔𝖑𝖚𝖒𝖊

IS INSCRIBED, WITH THE SINCERE AFFECTION AND ESTEEM

OF

THE AUTHOR.

CONTENTS.

	PAGE
Parkside Cottage,	1
Mally,	26
Courtin' Neet,	37
The Mountains,	41
Musings,	47
Birthday Sonnet,	51
Richard Cobden,	52
Richard Combden,	54
The Keeper's Son,	56
Maggie,	59
Little Child upon my Knee,	61
Song.—I Heave a Sigh for Thee,	64
Abraham Lincoln,	67

Contents.

	PAGE
Come, Sally,	71
Life's a Game,	74
My Johnny,	78
Consistent "Brown,"	82
On the Lake,	85
Christmas,	88
Man and Monkey,	93
The Blighted Flower,	96
Oh, What yet Unopened Chambers,	98
Encouragement,	101
Justice,	105
Music and Colours,	107
The Widower,	109
Praise not other Lands to Me,	114
I am Sad,	117
On a Late Spring,	120
Marriage,	122
Th' Sexton to his Spade,	123
The Old Year to a Little Girl,	126
Flowers,	128
To Little "Willie,"	130

Contents.

	PAGE
Sonnet,	136
Morning Hymn,	137
Praise,	139
"If I make my Bed in Hell, Behold, Thou art There,"	143
Marriages and Deaths,	150
Grief,	152
Lines on Returning a Pocket-Handkerchief to a Lady	155
A Valentine,	158
Lines to a Lady, with the Author's "Carte,"	160
Lines to a Lady who sent Her "Carte" to the Author,	162
Tinkle, Tinkle, Tiny Brooklet,	164
To my Mother,	167
The Man who is Kind to Another,	170
Welcome to Garibaldi,	173
I've Known the Rich Man Die,	179
I am a Little Valentine,	182

i

PARKSIDE COTTAGE.

PEACEFUL was the Sabbath morning,
　　Very full of peace and rest ;
Larks were singing high in heaven,
　　Each one singing out his best.

Many birds on leafy branches
　　Carol'd sweetly in the trees ;
Throstle, blackbird, linnet, pouring
　　Choral raptures on the breeze.

Flora listen'd to the music,
　　And beneath Sol's golden rays

Fill'd the air with sweetest odour,
    Joining incense to the praise.

Bees in very joy were humming,
    And the varied butterflies,
Animated little flowerets,
    Play'd among the melodies.

Peaceful cattle in the pastures
    Grazed, or lay upon the ground ;
While in other pastures near them
    Patient-looking sheep were found.

Woods, and fields, plains, hills, and valleys,
    All were bathed in golden sheen ;
And the sky was so transparent,
    That the heavens beyond were seen.

On the wings of languid south winds
    Came the sound of distant bells ;

Swinging, waving, back and forward,
   O'er the hills and through the dells.

And anon I heard the tinkle
   Of a little chapel bell,
Like a note that wanted tuning,
   And it sounded crack'd as well.

And I heard some little children
   Singing hymns, not far away,
And their sweet angelic praises
   Made me *feel* the Sabbath-day.

Then the music ceased, and nature
   Such a placid aspect wore!
It was like an infant sleeping,
   When the lullaby is o'er.

It was thuswise that I wander'd,
   On that Sabbath morn in June,

With a calm and restful spirit,
    And my feelings all in tune.

And my feet, as if by instinct,
    Found an unfrequented lane,
Over which the grass was growing,
    Making it a field again.

Oh, I like that quaint old pathway,
    For it speaks of days gone by,
When our grandsires used the packhorse,
    And to market thus would hie!

Ruts, where once the carts had travell'd,
    Left a rough, uneven ground;
But there was a charm about it
    That in highways is not found.

In the ditch that ran along it,
    Ferns were growing all the way,

And the many-colour'd wild-flowers
    Made the very ditch look gay.

And the hedges high above me
    Were luxuriously wild,
Shooting up in all directions,
    By the summer sun beguiled.

And an oak-tree, stooping stiffly
    O'er the ditch, in silence grew,
Looking like an aged woman
    Dress'd in garments bright and new.

Here, upon its roots, I rested,
    Shaded from the burning sun,
Listening to the richest concert
    That had e'er my spirit won.

For the singing of the song-birds
    In the hedges and the trees,

With the rippling of a brooklet,
    Were commingled by the breeze.

And the noble choral leader
    Of this concert in the air,
Pour'd his eloquence of praises
    On the beauties that were there.

While the fulness of my fancy
    Made me think I something heard
That was sweeter than the music
    Of the brooklet or the bird.

Oh, the wondrous charm of nature
    To the man who loves her well;
Who woos her, and, in loving,
    Feels a joy he cannot tell.

And, in holding sweet communion
    With the spirit of the fair,

Reads a thousand truths and beauties
    That another sees not there.

But I rose at last and wander'd
    On a road both clean and wide,
With its rows of oak and elm trees
    Marshall'd up on either side.

Through the which I got sweet glimpses
    Of the hills that rose afar,
Looking solemn in the distance,
    Clad in robes of sombre fir.

And I went along the highway
    To a stile, o'er which I strode,
Then along a narrow footpath,
    Past the "keeper's" neat abode.

It was sweet, along that pathway,
    Running through two fields of corn,

Parkside Cottage.

With the sun of June upon me
    On that peaceful Sabbath morn.

But I wander'd past the corn-fields,
    Through a gate, and kept my way
Down a gently-sloping meadow
    That had yielded up its hay.

Then I pass'd a farm, and onwards
    Through another narrow lane,
Till I came to Parkside Cottage,
    Where I oft shall go again.

Round the garden stood a hedgerow,
    Neatly trimm'd, but not too high,
Just to keep the garden private
    From the people passing by.

In the centre was a wicket
    Newly painted, and though small,

Had a look as if 'twould open
   With a welcome smile for all.

Here I stood a single minute,
   Took a survey of the place,
Saw the garden, neat and tidy,
   As a waiting lover's face.

Saw the little beds surrounded
   With the " box," that looks so well ;
Saw the little walks around them
   Paved with glistening oyster shell.

Saw the roses, many shaded,
   From the white to deeply red,
And the butterfly-like pansies,
   Peeping out of every bed.

And so many blooming beauties
   That were playing with the breeze,

And all laughing with the sunshine,
    Or coquetting with the bees.

That the garden was a "harem,"
    Where the loves delight to dwell,
Where the honey bees were lovers,
    And each blooming flower a "belle."

Parkside Cottage had been whitewashed,
    And its heavy thatch of straw
Made it look as neat a dwelling
    As in truth I ever saw.

Such a cot as lovers fancy,
    When their love is all in all;
Where they think they could be happy,
    And no evil could befall.

It was quaint, and snug, and pet-like,
    Homely as there are but few;

PARK SIDE COTTAGE.

It was quaint, and snug, and pet-like,
  Homely as there are but few,
Chubby-faced, and plump, and rosy,
  Doubled-chinned, and dimpled too.

Chubby-faced, and plump, and rosy,
    Double-chinn'd and dimpled too.

Ay! it seem'd the very figure
    Of a happy parent's joy,
Or the crystallised affection
    Of a mother for her boy.

It was home spell'd out in letters
    That affection knows alone,
And it seem'd as if *not builded*,
    But to form of home had *grown*.

It had two snug bedroom windows,
    That were very small in size,
And the thatch waved nicely o'er them
    Just like "brows" o'er laughing eyes.

Round the windows down below them
    There were rose-trees full of bloom,

Parkside Cottage.

And like bashful swains, the roses
   Peep'd and nodded in the room.

And the thatch'd porch round the doorway
   Seem'd just fitted to its place,
And was like a hood with ribbons
   Round a bonny baby's face.

But the cottage altogether,
   Deeply set among the trees,
Seem'd the very spot where Cupid
   Would find home, and be at ease.

Never such another cottage
   Have I in my rambles seen;
Such a very pearl of beauty
   Set in living em'rald green.

Now, I did not know the inmates,
   But I felt as sure as fate,

They'd be something like the cottage,
   So I ventured through the gate.

And across the little garden
   Having made my silent way,
I reach'd the door within the porch,
   That appear'd in words to say :

" If thou canst speak our shibboleth,
   Which is peace and good to all,
Then enter; but if thou canst not,
   Then, stranger, do not call."

So I enter'd, for my spirit
   . Was as peaceful and serene
As a maiden's, who to vespers
   On a summer's eve had been.

There was not a hall or lobby,
   As in mansions of the great,

Where a stranger, *like a stranger*,
   For the master's will must wait.

But the doorway led directly
   To the very heart of home,
And the floor so white and sanded—
   Seem'd to whisper to me—"Come."

And the cat that lay upon it,
   Stretch'd and sleeping in the sun,
Did not heed me or my coming,
   But continued sleeping on.

And the "settle" just before me,
   In its check of blue and white,
With its back of oak, well polish'd,
   Seem'd my presence to invite.

Now the rich man has his sofa,
   Or his couch or easy-chair,

But there's nothing to my thinking
   With the "settle" will compare.

For it seems as if old Comfort,
   Fill'd it up so round and high,
That the aches of all creation
   It was ready to defy.

Oh, I love the quaint old "settle,"
   On a white and sanded floor,
In a homely English cottage,
   Ay, the cottage of the poor!

Not the sofas or the couches,
   On their carpets e'er can be,
In the truest sense of comfort,
   What the "settle" seems to me.

Just above this ancient "settle,"
   In a polish'd rosewood frame,

Was a picture done in wool-work—
   And beneath, the worker's name.

In the window was a flower-pot,
   Fill'd with musk, whose sweet perfume,
As with incense from an altar,
   Fill'd the humble little room.

Round the window hung a valance,
   Trim'd with fringe, and all so white,
That a lily of the valley
   Is not purer to the sight.

On the mantelpiece, in order,
   Were some ornaments for show,
While the fire, as if in protest,
   Burn'd with dull and sulky glow.

But the old man, who was sitting
   In his high-back'd, two-armed chair,

Was the most attractive object,
    And the noblest that was there.

He was old, as age is measured
    By the length of time he'd told;
And his brave, broad back was bended,
    Like the fading leaves that fold.

But his eye was clear and candid,
    And as peaceful and serene
As the star that in the grayness
    Of the eventime is seen.

And his hair was like the moonlight
    That by fairies had been spun
Into slender cords for stringing
    Old Time's rosaries upon.

And his brow was broad, and cover'd
    With deep hieroglyphs of care;

But beside them and around them
    There were marks of honour there.

He was like a brave old soldier
    Who had laid his weapons by,
And was waiting the commander,
    To reward his bravery.

He was list'ning, as I enter'd,
    To the reading of a child,
From that good old Book, the Bible;
    And at times the old man smiled.

I disturbed them for a little;
    And old Joseph raised his head;
But I join'd them in the worship,
    While that little priestess read.

And my soul had sweet communion
    With the Father who was there;

And that room became a temple
   Where my spirit knelt in prayer.

And if e'er a place was hallow'd
   With the incense of sweet praise,
It was when "Amen" was utter'd
   By that patriarch of days.

Oh! there's something in religion
   That is pure and undefiled,
That may baffle all the learned,—
   Yet be simple to the child.

Now the old man in his cottage
   Was not learned, but was wise,
And methinks where some are lacking
   He will one day take a prize.

Little "Jessie" who was reading
   Was his daughter's latest born,

And he loved to have her with him—
    It was evening's thought of morn.

Fourscore years and *four* are kindred,
    Age and childhood are allied,
He was Winter, she was Spring-time,
    Snow and snow-drop side by side.

She was light was little Jessie,
    Quite a Saxon, very fair,
With a round and ample forehead
    Underneath smooth flaxen hair.

She was very like what Joseph
    With his face smooth'd out would be,
And she minded me of *new wood*
    Sprouting from an aged tree.

Little thing, she loved her grandsire,
    And would rather read than play,

If he would but kiss her for it,
   And "God bless thee!" to her say.

And what eyes were little Jessie's,
   Like an eagle's, black and bright,
With a dashing sparkle in them
   Like a shooting-star at night.

And old Joseph's eyes were like them,
   Only cavern'd deep in years,
And they'd lost their greatest lustre
   In the bath of sorrow's tears.

And what cheeks had little Jessie,
   Lily-white, with rosy bloom,
While the old man's cheeks were shrivell'd,
   Folded ready for the tomb.

Jessie's face was like a garden,
   Full of all the flowers of spring,

With the hedges newly budding,
    In which throstles sweetly sing.

But the old man's was a garden,
    Where the winter long had been,
Cover'd o'er with winter's surplice,
    But wreath'd o'er with evergreen.

She was reading from the Psalmist,
    He who sang in ancient days,
Who, when bearing crook and sceptre,
    Sang alike the Maker's praise.

And she read about the Shepherd,
    Who in pastures green and fair,
And beside the peaceful waters,
    Led His flocks with tender care.

And she read about the traveller,
    Who, without a fear of ill,

Walk'd the valley dark with shadows,
   For the Lord was with him still.

Aye His rod and staff were comfort,
   And His goodness led the way,
And a faith He gave the traveller,
   That the darkness led to day.

And the old man, list'ning calmly,
   With his elbows on his chair,
And his snow-white head low bending,
   Knew that he must soon prepare

For the walking of that valley,
   And he gave a long deep sigh,
Not of murmur or repining,
   'Twas a prayer that went on high ;

And a tear there was escaped him,
   That on coming from his eye,

Took its course along a furrow
   That from tears had long been dry;

It was slow, as if unwilling
   To depart that long-loved home,
And it halted, as if striving
   'Gainst the parting that must come.

But it fell at last, and mixing
   With the sand upon the floor,
In the sun a while it glisten'd,
   Then the tear's first life was o'er.

But I thought an angel took it
   To her bosom, where it grew,
From a tear-drop to a diamond,
   As the tears of mortals do.

And the angel kept the jewel
   For the crown that should be worn

By that aged weeping pilgrim
   When to heaven he should be borne.

And the angel waited for him,
   Like a mother for her son,
Who, his school-days being ended,
   Wish'd his nobler life begun.

MALLY.

WHEN fust aw seed thee, Mally, lass,
    Theaw knows 'twur near th' owd ho'
I' Weshbruck-lone, tort Witches-neest,
    Wheere th' cloof runs deawn below :
'Twur summer toime, an' th' honey bees
    Could sing, but dar no' play,
An' th' breezes mixt a theawsand smells
    O fleawrs an' leaves wi' hay.

The corn had reicht its youthfu' days,
    An' stood booath strung an' hee,
Whoile th' cattle grazed i' meadows green,
    Wi' new shorn sheep just nee ;

An' th' swallows leetly skimm'd o'er th' ponds,
    Then derted quick away,
Whoile th' layruck, fairly cawt o seet,
    Wur singin a' th' lung day;

An' th' ferns an' wild fleawrs deawn ith cloof,
    An' th' velvet mosses too,
Loike nayburs on a holiday,
    Seem'd donn'd i' dresses new;
An' th' pratty little tinklin' bruck—
    A babby uv a stream—
Play'd music as it toddled on,
    As sweet as love's fust dream.

My hert wur reetly tuned for love;
    An' when aw lookt on thee
Aw felt as if aw'd just fun cawt
    Wot heaven itsel mun be.
Aw're stonnin just at th' eend oth cloof—
    'Twur Sunday afternoon,

An' th' Prestwich bells wur singin' eawt
    Their prattiest Sunday tune.

Aw felt as if a' th' summer toime
    Wur bloomin' i' my breast,
Wi' th' fleawrs, an' trees, an' brids, an' brucks,
    An' sunsheighne, an' a' th' rest.
Thy face wur th' sun, an' aw wur th' greawnd;
    Ay, Mally, it wur so;
An' a' th' good seeds sown i' my breast
    Wur made by thee to grow.

Aw seed thy leet an' curly yure,
    Aw seed thy soft blue een,
Aw seed thy rosy dimpled cheeks
    Wi' kissin' lips between;
An' theaw wur donn'd up i' thy best—
    Theaw lookt so foine an' shy—
Theaw'd got new shoon--aw seed thy foot
    Peep eawt so peert an' sly.

Aw dursn't speighk, aw could bo' look,
   Bo' when theaw 'd pass'd me by,
Aw follow'd on, as near 's aw dar,
   An' heighved up mony a soigh ;
Bo' when theaw geet to th' eend oth lone,
   Aw turn'd for th' " Top o' Stond ;"
Aw brast'd off as if aw 're feort—
   By th' mass, aw did clear th' lond.

Eh ! but aw wur some takken in,
   It wur a bonny go,
Aw fun thee speighkin snug enoof
   An' lowfin wi' lung Joe.
A' th' steom shot off i' hawve a crack,
   Aw 're loike a brid i' rain,
Aw thowt theaw wur his sweethert, lass,
   So aw slunk whoam ogen.

'Twur th' feawst walk aw ever had,
   Though sitch a pratty day ;

Aw seed nowt noice, not aw indeed,
    But purr'd aw th' stones ith way.
Aw hung my yed an' welly cried,
    An' wur so gradely mad,
An' bote my lips, an' knit my brees,
    An' then turn'd soppin sad.

Aw 'd getten cleawds insoide o' me,
    My day wur turn'd to neet;
Aw 're cromm'd so full o' derkness then,
    There wur no reawm for leet.
A' th' seawnds aw yerd wur mufiled uns,
    Just loike a berryin bell;
Aw'd sitch a naught an' dummy feel,
    So numb aw conno tell.

My mother axt me wot wur t' do—
    Hoo thowt aw mut be ill—
An' made some gruel, spoiced an' noice,
    An' browt a doctor's pill.

Mally.

But that ud do no good, nor it,
    It noane cures th' hert o' woe;
Bo' aw thowt if aw could ha my will
    Aw'd give a pill to Joe.

Well, aw fret aw day, an' rowlt aw neet,
    Abeawt a wick or two,
An' then my mother fun me cawt,
    An' said aw wur a foo.
Hoo towd me t' goo an' speighk to th' lass,
    An' get it some road o'er;
Mak th' job a kiss or else a miss;
    But dunno lay on th' floor.

Hoo met as weel ha spoke to th' pump—
    Aw know'd naught wot hoo said;
Bo' then my fayther coom, by th' mass!
    An' he cleawted me o'er th' yed.
Owd lass, that gaen me sitch a stert,
    Aw jumpt reet off my cheor;

Th' owd pluck coom back; aw show'd for feight:
    As if aw'd had t' mitch beer.

Then mother lowft, an' fayther lowft,
    An' said, " Goo lad eawr Dick ;
He's getten th' foo's cap on at last ;
    Poor lad, he's turnt love sick."
Aw felt as soft as buttermilk,
    Bo' wot wur th' wust uv a',
Aw're welly lowfin cawt mysel,
    They aw wur lowfin so.

Next day my fayther made me wurtch,
    An', laws, it helpt me on,
Aw're better, but aw wurno weel,
    For th' hert wertch hadno gone.
Well, th' summer past, an' autumn toime,
    An' some oth winter too ;
When thee an' me we met at last
    Ith little chapel skoo.

Theaw knows 'twur th' Kesmus pertyin,
   An' after th' tay wur done,
An' th' speighkin, an' recoitin too,
   Waw th' doancin' wur begun.
Awst ne'er forget that neet, owd lass,
   For when aw doanced wi' thee,
Thy hont i' moine, an' moine i' thoine,
   Eh! 'twur gradely o'er wi' me.

Theaw recollects aw towd my tale,
   Aw did so soft, loike, feel;
'Twur done i' little bits an' scraps;
   But eh, theaw pieced um weel.
Theaw didno say theaw'd ha me then;
   Bo' sayin' naught wurn't no;
Theaw blusht aboon a bit, theaw did,
   An' hung thy yed so low.

We perted, an' aw sterted whoam,
   But aw'd no sleep that neet,

Aw're loike a dug lost in a fair,
    No soide nor place wur reet.
Aw're up at two o'clock ith morn
    An' off to th' Heeur-lone,
An' stood—a silly foo's aw wur—
    Beneath thy window stone.

Bo' never moind, aw'll say no mooar.
    'Twur a' made reet at last;
An' sin' that toime full mony a day
    Uv happiness we'n past.
Its noice to turn us reawnd a bit
    An' look at days gone by.
Let's hutch together, Mally, woife,
    Loike cleawds ith sunset sky.

Owd love is loike to th' roipened fruit:
    Yung love loike th' bloomin is;
We'n tasted, an' we loike um booath,
    Theyn' each their sort o' bliss.

"It's noice to turn us reawnd a bit
   An' look at days gone by."—Page 34.

Mally.

Eawr coortin days are past and gone,
   But love ull never quit ;
Let's put my arm reet reawnd thy waist,
   An' closer to thee sit.

Neaw lay thy yed uppo my breast,
   As t' did i' "owd lang syne ;"
One hond shall stroke thy wrinkled cheek,
   Whoile t' other's held i' thoine ;
An' let us shut cawr een un dream
   Uv yunger days an' spring.
Nay, dunno cry, owd lass, or else
   Th' brids in us winno sing.

God bless thee, Mally ! good owd woife !
   Love doesno dee wi yers ;
But, see, awve brokken deawn mysel ;
   Let's mix cawr bits o' tears :
They winno speighl cawt, will they, lass ?
   They're but late April sheawrs ;

We'st foind cawr May toime up aboon ;
    These tears ull help thoose fleawrs.

Awm satisfied wi' th' loife we'n had,
    An' thankfu' for it, too,
Although we'n wawkt o'er roofish roads
    An' pood up mony a broo.
We'n gone through every lond ith world,
    Booath woot an' cowd an' o' ;
Sometoimes been melted deawn wi' heat,
    An' sometoimes smoort wi' snow.

But, lookin' back, it's plain enoof
    'Twur nobbut shade an' leet,
To make up th' pictur' o' one's loife—
    It shows ut aw comes reet.
Bo lift thy yed, neaw, Mally, woife.
    Toime's slippin' fast away ;
Let's up, an' do that bit o' werk
    There's left for th' close o' day.

COURTIN' NEET.

WEDNESDAY looks like th' longest day,
  An' wark is hard to do ;
Dirt seems to stick to everythin',
  Aw scarcely con get through.
It's just as if the boggarts coom
  To set things all awry ;
Aw conna get 'em lookin' reet,
  Hewever mich aw try.
      It's courtin' neet, it's courtin' neet,
        My heart's so full o' glee ;
      There's not a neet like this i' th' week,
        When Robin comes to me.

This morn' aw're weshing th' breakfast things,
    An' singing to mysel',
When th' cream-jug tumbled upo th' floor,
    An' broke because it fell.
An' just as if that weren't enoof
    To give a crayter fits,
Aw bump'd my yed when stoopin' doun
    To pick up th' broken bits.
        It's courtin' neet, it's courtin' neet, &c.

Well, then aw started makin' the beds,
    Just same's aw allus do;
But th' blankets geet where th' sheets should be,
    An' the pillows geet wrang too.
The dule seem'd getten houd o' th' bed,
    An' everythin' beside;
Aw couldna get 'em lookin' reet,
    However mich aw tried.
        It's courtin' neet, it's courtin' neet, &c.

Aw never have been gradely reet
  Sin Robin towd me true,
Ut my black een an' curly yure
  Had made him sich a foo'.
Aw never know'd my een were black
  Till Robin towd me so;
But as he likes 'em black, aw wish
  They'd ten times blacker grow.
    It's courtin' neet, it's courtin' neet, &c.

But now aw think aw've fairly done,
  An', finish'd up for th' day,
Aw've donn'd me i' my Sunday best,
  An' feel as fine as May.
Aw do wish Robin ud come now,
  Aw'm just so full o' glee,
Aw'm sure aw should go reet to heaven
  If now aw were to dee.
    It's courtin' neet, it's courtin' neet, &c.

But time's so queer, it allus goes
    Too fast or else too slow;
If e'er it knows what folks do want,
    Th' wrung pace it's sure to go.
It's plagued me mony a time, it has,
    But if aw'd got my will,
Aw'd mak it fly till Robin coom,
    And then it should stond still.
        It's courtin' neet, it's courtin' neet, &c.

THE MOUNTAINS.

SUGGESTED BY THE VIEW FROM MATSON HILL,
BOWNESS, WESTMORELAND.

OH, the massive, mighty mountains,
   How majestically grand,
In their solitary greatness,
   Full of dignity they stand—
Rearing up their heads so proudly,
   Like the monarchs of the land.

Look at yonder splendid mountains,
   Range on range and peak on peak,
" Black Comb," " Langdale Pikes," and " Orrest,"

With the " Old Man," dark and bleak,
And the distant stranger mountains,
　　Stretching up as if to speak.

If thou e'er hast seen the billows
　　Of the mighty ocean rise,
And beheld old Neptune's bosom,
　　Heaving grandly towards the skies,
Tell me if these awful mountains
　　Are not storm-waves in disguise?

Oh, the everlasting mountains!
　　Solitary and sublime,
Calm and dignified, and stately
　　As the Titans in their prime,
Great Leviathans of ocean
　　Stranded in the ancient time.

Like a bed of billows are they,
　　For the night to rest upon,
Trackless as the boundless ocean,

Pathway of the Great Unknown.
  Solemn as the rolling thunder
When the lightning dart is thrown.

Solemn are the towering mountains,
  When the night in silence throws
Darkness round them as a garment,
  Fold on fold as daylight goes,
Till it seemeth like a chamber
  Of Goliaths in repose.

Solemn is the hour of midnight,
  Whether on the sea or land;
But if on some great high mountain
  At the witching hour we stand,
It becomes sublimely solemn—
  It becomes intensely grand.

Or if night's pale queen is shining,
  With the stars that weave their light
Into gossamer-like veilings

For the placid face of night,
Then the mountains seem like dreamland,
To which Fancy takes her flight.

Oh, the sight among the mountains!
When the sun is sinking low,
And the western sky is burning
With a molten-golden glow—
Like a sea of living glory
Into which all splendours flow.

And the clouds from out the eastward
Crowd above that they may view
That sumptuousness of splendour,
As the pageant passes through,
And they catch a glow of glory
As all heavenward gazers do.

While the mountain-tops are halo'd
With a brilliant golden sheen,
And the lights and shadows mingling

The Mountains.

In the valleys down between,
Throw a mellow tone of purple
   O'er the sombre heather green.

Or perhaps below the mountain,
   In some pass or ravine, where
Rocks are hiding all but heaven,
   And no sounds disturb the air,
Save the breezes far above me,
   Like the angels winging there.

Oh, 'tis then I love to see them!
   In the peaceful evening calm,
When the atmosphere of summer
   Is a nectar and a balm,
And the silence e'en is music
   That is echo'd in a psalm.

And 'tis then that I would worship
   In that temple all alone,
With no priest to stand between me

And the mighty God I own,
And no sound except the night-winds
As day's requiem they intone.

For methinks the Great Eternal,
Who is present everywhere,
And whose throne is all creation,
Would yet show me He was there,
And as though it were a " Patmos,"
Would His mysteries declare.

MUSINGS.

'TIS sweet to walk at eventide
　　Through narrow lanes or pastures wide,
To tread the vale or climb the hill,
Or muse beside the rippling rill,
Or watch the daisies close their eyes;
While Sol, in all his glory dies,
And sinks beneath the western sea
To rise where morn shall waiting be.
Yet ere he leaves us quite away,
Lighting the moon with pearly ray,
Bidding her reign the queen of night,
Shedding abroad her pensive light,
Silvering every leaf and spray
Along the weary traveller's way,

Wooing the tender nightingale
To tell her sweet love-laden tale,
While all the world beside is still,
As listening to that heavenly trill.

'Tis sweet to walk the forest through,
Where shadows come ere night is due,
And where e'en in the height of day
Light reaches but in broken ray,
And lies upon the mossy ground
Like treasure-fragments all around.
'Tis sweet to see the waving fern
Kiss'd by the breeze at every turn ;
And wild flowers nearly hid from view,
Lifting their heads for kisses too ;
While brave old trees look down to see
The little folks so full of glee.

'Tis sweet to walk the river-side,
And watch the ever-flowing tide ;

To meet the stream, or keep its way,
Or thoughtful on its banks to stay:
While playful fishes swimming by,
Dart up to catch the heedless fly.
'Tis sweet, indeed, to sit and hear
The water-music, soft and clear;
As if the genii of the glade,
Had magic harps of water made;
And strung them with the sun's bright rays,
To give the glorious summer praise.

Oh! doubly sweet, if by my side
Some loved one listens to the tide;
And we together sit and muse,
Till summer does our souls suffuse
With summer love and summer calm,
And joy and peace, our souls embalm.
'Tis sweeter than the tongue can tell,
With those we dearly love to dwell;

While beauty, though most passing fair,
Is nothing, if love be not there.
'Tis sweet, all lovely things to see ;
But love makes all things fair to be.

BIRTHDAY SONNET.

OH! days and deeds, life's warp and woof,
   Weave on, weave on, and clear the loom!
Mine's but a coarse, plain-pattern'd web,
Yet needed in the great stock-room.
The Master gave the work to me,
And meted with it power and skill;
He knew what all the web would be,
And yet to send me was His will.
Oh! Master, where I've marr'd the work,
Thou know'st I've wept and tried again;
My blundering has taught me skill;
My errors have not been in vain;
And Thou hast taught me this strange song,
We learn the right by doing wrong.

RICHARD COBDEN.

DIED, APRIL 2, 1865.

O DEATH! thou hast been hard with us to-day.
    Didst thou not stagger ere this deed was done?
So good a life thou canst not often stay;
Thy stroke has ta'en from England's heart a *Son!*
Grim monster, turn, and see what thou hast done.
Surely the sight of that still countenance,
That temple where the truth was wont to dwell;
That frozen summer—mansion tenantless,
That tree, fruit-laden, on which winter fell,
Shall make e'en thy hard breast with sorrow swell.

Death! weep thou with us, if thou hast one tear
Left in thy dark and deeply-cavern'd eye.
Yet go!—thou didst thy worst—and still he lives;
He gave his life, and so can never die!

RICHARD COBDEN.

DIED, APRIL 2, 1865.

HE sought not glory, nor yet courted fame,
    A patriot was he, loving England well;
His deeds have added splendour to her name:
His words, like diamonds, on her greatness fell;
All honour to one who could so excel!
The people's sorrows made him ever strong,
His country's follies made him blush for shame:
He wept before the poor man's cruel wrong,
But lighted such a fierce and searching flame,
As burn'd that blackness out of England's fame.

He fought and conquer'd for the people's good ;
And earth no monument for him can raise
So beautiful as his own rectitude,
And poor men's wailings that he changed to praise.

THE KEEPER'S SON.

No braver lad e'er walk'd the wood,
    No fairer lad could be
Than Johnny Brown, the keeper's son,
    Who lived at Walker Lea.
Shouldering gun, he forth would go,
    Nor tire the longest day,
With faithful "Don" close up "to heel,"
    His work was always play.

They'd wander through the wooded glen,
    Or climb the mountain high,
They'd cross the stubble fields and creep
    As softly as a sigh.

The Keeper's Son.

And if a bird should chance to rise,
   Or rabbit dare to run,
'Twould surely fall beneath the shot
   Of Johnny's fatal gun.

One morn with faithful "Don" he went,
   ('Twas in October's chill,)
To get a little early sport,
   Beneath the western hill;
When firing at a brace of birds,
   And thinking all was well,
The gun it burst, and on the ground
   The bleeding sportsman fell.

All senseless on the ground he lay,
   But "Don" was by his side,
And when he saw his master bleed,
   The faithful dog he cried.
He lick'd the wounds with tender care,
   Then by his side he lay,

To keep his master's body warm,
    On that October day.

'Twas very sad, for on that night,
    At dusk, John did agree,
To meet the miller's daughter Jane,
    Beneath the chestnut-tree.
She went and waited, but alas!
    She waited all in vain,
And tears were falling down her cheeks,
    As home she walk'd again.

The wound was fatal, and poor John,
    He never breathèd more;
And Jane she could not love again,
    But widow's weeds she wore.
The dog and she together live,
    And day by day they go,
To see the spot where Johnny Brown,
    The Keeper's son, lies low.

MAGGIE.

OH, thou bonny rose-lipp'd lassie,
    More than roses thou must be,
For the month of rosy beauty
    Is but March compared with thee.
        My love Maggie,
        Sweetheart Maggie,
    All the flowers thou art to me.

Yet the flowers of field or garden,
    Breathing fragrance on the breeze,
Or the birds that carol sweetly,
    Making concert in the trees.

My love Maggie,
Sweetheart Maggie,
These have not thy power to please.

My poor heart was cold and barren,
Cold as winter and as drear,
Until thou, by smiling on me,
Gav'st me summer all the year.
My love Maggie,
Sweetheart Maggie,
Flowers must bloom when thou art near.

Summer-time, and spring, and autumn,
All their mantles o'er thee fling;
Laureate art thou to the seasons,
Praising, loving everything.
My love Maggie,
Sweetheart Maggie,
Queen thou art, oh, make me king.

LITTLE CHILD UPON MY KNEE.

LITTLE child upon my knee,
　　Say not that we yet have done;
Turn thy smiling face to me,
　　Like the sunflower to the sun,
　　For more kisses I have won.

Little child upon my knee,
　　Let me stroke thy curly hair,
Falling down so carelessly,
　　Graceful as laburnums are,
　　But a thousand times more fair.

Little child upon my knee,
　　Let my arms around thee fold,

Like the ivy round a tree—
  Closely—and the Winter's cold
  We'll defy, for Love is bold.

Little child upon my knee,
  Look into my face, I pray,
And my love shall shine on thee,
  As the sun does all the day,
  On the baby flowers of May.

Sweetie, kneel upon my knee,
  Round my neck thy arms entwine;
Show how much thou lovest me;
  Say how much of love is mine,
  All my heart, dear child, is thine.

Little birdie on my knee,
  Wilt thou something for me sing,
Like a linnet in a tree;
  Not like skylark on the wing;
  Something very simple sing

Little child upon my knee,
   Now thy years are very few :
Count them, dearie,—one—two—three ;
   Oh, thou art so bright and new,
   And thou art so bonny too.

Little child upon my knee,
   Would that I could keep thee pure ;
But there is One keepeth thee,
   And His love is very sure,
   And His care does aye endure.

Thou art on *that* Father's knee,
   And if He'd no child beside,
He couldn't love more tenderly,
   Nor be to thee a surer Guide ;
   Sweet one, in His bosom hide.

SONG.

I HEAVE A SIGH FOR THEE.

MARY, when comes the evening,
    With calm and mellow light,
When golden clouds like pillows,
    Lie on the bed of night;
When the air is calm and still,
    And scarce a breeze moves by,
'Tis then, my dark-eyed Mary,
    I heave for thee a sigh.

When the birds have sung their vespers,
    And hid themselves away,

Song.—I Heave a Sigh for Thee.

While their heads are snugly folded
   Beneath their wings till day;
When the evening star of love
   Looks down with pensive eye,
'Tis then, my dark-eyed Mary,
   I heave for thee a sigh.

When the summer sun arises,
   And meets the waiting morn,
While the sparkling dew rejoices,
   Another day is born;
And the sharp and bracing air
   Gives life in passing by,
'Tis then, my dark-eyed Mary,
   I heave for thee a sigh.

Through all the changing seasons,
   Through every night and day,
Where'er my feet may wander,
   In work, or rest, or play,

My heart is still with thee,
    And will be till I die.
Oh! come, be mine, then, Mary,
    And stay this heaving sigh.

ABRAHAM LINCOLN,

ASSASSINATED APRIL 14, 1865.

THE deed is done! and God who reigns above
  Staid not the hand—nor took its power away.
It "needs must be;" but was there no less crime
That could epitomise, or clearly write,
And show, as in a fixèd statue form,
The real hideousness of that great wrong
Which fought for mastery on earth, but fell
Ulcer'd with curses to the very core?

Foul though the deed, most execrably foul,
Ugly alike in sight of Earth and Heaven,

Without a parallel—so steep'd in sin ;
Yet hath the power of God from out the ill
Brought forth such good, and caused the wrath of man
To give Him such high praise, that those who see
Adore ! and marvel at the Providence
That so controls and governs in the world.

I once beheld a vase, so beautiful,
So perfect in its form and ornament,
That e'en the vulgar, looking on't, refined ;
But in a seeming evil hour, a fool
Broke it to spite the owner ; when there came
From out the shatter'd fragments such a cloud
Of rich perfume, that e'en the fool himself
Shed tears at finding what he had reveal'd.

So is it here. This great and dark offence,—
This cruel sin, has proved a sacrifice
From which doth rise such incense, that the world
Is fill'd, as a great temple, with perfume,
While God accepts Earth's sacrifice, and smiles.

Never did human hate so perfectly
Compel the flowing of Celestial love,
Nor harsh discordances awake to life
Sweet harmonies, as this one deed has done.
From it shall grow a tree—so large,
So strong, so beautiful, and full of fruit,
That underneath its branches myriads dwell
In full-grown liberty, who once were slaves,
And none shall dare to make them fear again.

Lincoln, thy name shall live! and from thy death
The martyr glory gathers round thy brow;
Thy country, not thyself, was ever first
In all thy thoughts, and Patriot is thy name!
The truth—the simple truth—so loved by thee,
Shall crystallise and form thy monument.
Thy life was fatal to oppression's rule!
Thy death is resurrection to the slave!
Thy memory is embalmed within the hearts
Of millions as a very precious thing!

And Negro children, in the years to come,
Shall learn to talk by speaking first thy name ;
While aged mothers, in their dying hours,
Shall whisper " Lincoln " as they pass away.

COME, SALLY.

COME, Sally, come in to thy supper,
    It 's time to be goin' to bed,
For when tha were gettin' thy baggin',
    Tha talk'd of a pain i' thy yed.

Eh, mother, aw 'm listenin' to th' corncrake,
    Ut's scrapin' its throat near yon hill,
It strikes upo' th' air like a clock tick,
    At midneet, when everythin 's still.
Some leaves upo' th' trees are just movin'
    Like folk at turn o'er i' their sleep,
An' silvery white clouds are sailin'
    Like angels ut watch o'er 'em keep.

Why, Sally, tha'r losin' thy senses—
    Tha shouldna be turnin' a foo,
Aw've made thee a plate o' meal porritch,
    Come in then, an' tak it, lass do.

Eh, mother, aw 'm lookin' at th' moonleet,
    It's prattiest neet e'er aw seed,
An' th' yedache has melted i' th' stillness,
    An' th' supper aw durnt feel to need.
Put th' porritch i' th' cupboard till mornin',
    Warm'd up it'll do reet for me,
But, mother, aw 'm fain to be cawt now,
    It's bonniest neet yo could see.

Why, Sally, tha shouldna be simple,
    Tha'r surely forgettin' its late,
An' th' porritch clouds rise up to th' ceilin'
    As if t' invite thee to eayt.

Nay, mother, aw winna come in yet,
    An' couldna goo t' bed if aw did,

Bu' tha'd better goo if tha 'r wantin',
    Aye just do for once as tha 'r bid.
Bu' lemme stop cawt a bit longer,
    Aw couldna be happy inside,
For the moonleet fa's down upo' th' roses,
    As nice as a veil o'er a bride.

Well, well then, aw'll bid thee good neet lass,
    Bu' dunna thee stop cawt so long,
Or else tha'll be gettin' a cowd like,
    For, Sally, tha art na so strong.

Good neet, my owd mother, God bless thee!
    Aw'll come to thy side in a while,
Bu' now aw'll be off to my sweetheart,
    Aw know he'll be waitin' at th' stile.
Aw didna tell lees about th' moonleet,
    It's prattiest neet yo could see,
Though aw wouldna stop cawt o' my bed for't
    If Johnny weren't waitin' for me.

LIFE'S A GAME.

LIFE'S a game, and all are playing;
    Some are winning, others lose—
But the truth is told in saying,
All have power to win who choose.
Let us only be in earnest,
Using all our wit and skill,
And whate'er the game of life be,
We can win it if we will.
    Play it well, and play it bravely;
    Let the heart the hand impel;
    Whatsoe'er the game of life be,
    Play it wisely, play it well.

Life's a Game.

All men have a game of " cricket,"
That in youth well play'd should be,
Guarding virtue as a *wicket*,
With the *bat* of purity.
Some a game of " chess " are playing
'Gainst deceit and wrong within :—
Let them, ever *watching*, *praying*,
Mark each *move*, and they shall win.
  Play it well, and play it bravely.

Some a game of " whist " are playing,
With the " ace of hearts " in hand,
'Gainst the world's trump, " ace of diamonds ; "
But the true *heart* shall command.
Some men are at " croquet " playing—
May be *red* against the *blue*—
Let them scorn the *dizzie shaffle*,
And with honour play red through.
  Play it well, and play it bravely.

Some a game of "draughts" are playing,
And with most, some *men* have gone;
But the clear and cautious player
Crowns, and takes his *two for one*.
Others play a game of "billiards"
On their *life's-board*, smooth and true—
But to *cannon* or to *pocket*,
Steady hands must guide the *cue*.
  Play it well, and play it bravely.

Some a game of "risk" are playing—
"Speculation," "dice," or "loo;"
But it is not *chance*, for surely
Every one of them shall "*rue*."
Yet an *honest purpose* merely
Will not win the *game* we play;
We must be both wise and prudent,
If the prize we'd take away.
  Play it well, and play it bravely.

Life's a Game.

We must strive to be *proficient*
In our game, and e'en excel ;
And remember that *one false move*
Mars what else were play'd right well.
Move by *move* we should be cautious,
Making sure each one is right—
And whate'er the game of life be,
We shall win it ere the night.
      Play it well, and play it bravely

MY JOHNNY.

MY Johnny is the bonniest lad
    Ut lives i' Rachda Town,
His een are blue, his cheeks are red,
    His curly yure is brown,
He walks so like a gentleman,
    One yet aw 'm sure he'll be,
Aw am some proud to walk wi' him,
    An' let a' th' neighbours see.

An' then he's gettin' larnt i' books,
    An' reads a' th' papers too,

An' when he comes a courtin' me,
    He tells me all ut's new.
He sends a letter now and then,
    An' writes outside it, " Miss,"
An' as it comes instead o' John,
    It alus gets a kiss.

He warks i' th' factory, an' if those
    Ut wear his wark but knew,
What sort o' chap the weyver wur,
    They'd love it same's aw do.
They'd nobbut wear't on better days,
    Then lay it nicely by.
John mixes love wi' everythin',
    An' mae's bread taste like pie.

On Sunday when aw goo to church,
    An' get set nicely down,
Aw never know what th' parson says,
    My heart's i' Rachda Town.

But Johnny comes i' th' afternoon,
    An' never speaks i' vain,
Aw swallow every word he says,
    Like thirsty flowers drink rain.

Aw like to yer at th' cuckoo sing,
    In weepin' April's days;
Aw like to look at the layrock rise,
    An' scatter down his praise;
Aw like to stand i' th' quiet lone,
    While dayleet passes by;
But more by th' hauve nor these aw like
    To yer my Johnny sigh.

Oh, happy me, oh, lucky me,
    To have a chap like John;
He says aw'm th' nicest lass i' th' world,
    Aw'm sure he's th' finest mon.
He hasn't got a single fault,
    An's far too good for me,

My Johnny.

But as my Johnny loves me so,
    My very best aw'll be.

He says he's puttin' money by
    To get a house for me,
An' when he's gotten brass enoof,
    He says we wed mun be.
Aw dunnot like to think o' that,
    An' yet it's gradely true,
To be John's sweetheart a' my life
    Aw think ud hardly do.

CONSISTENT "BROWN."

EVER have I held one creed,
    Only one thing do I plead;
Need the truth in words be told,
That I worship only gold?
    "Bubble, bubble, toil and trouble,"
    If the gold it does not double,
    Into the caldron all goes down,
    For am I not consistent Brown?

Principles are only tools,
They who use them not are fools;
Everything we have should pay,
Or be quickly thrown away.
    Bubble, bubble, &c.

In my green and early youth,
Orthodoxy was my truth,
But it didn't pay at all,
So I sent it to the wall.
    Bubble, bubble, &c.

Then the Unitarian creed,
Tried to satisfy my greed,
But it didn't pay me long,
So I had to prove it wrong.
    Bubble, bubble, &c.

Then the Bible had to go,
For I found it didn't do,
As it blesses all the poor,
And poverty I can't endure.
    Bubble, bubble, &c.

Now I'm back to church again,
'Twill pay me better now than then ;

Verily, I'll preach and pray,
Just as long as folks will pay.
    Bubble, bubble, &c.

What I shall be ere I die,
You can't tell, friends, nor can I;
But you needn't this be told—
That I've always *change for gold*.
    Bubble, bubble, &c.

ON THE LAKE.

ANNIE, let us on the water,
   Now that evening meets the day,
As thou meetest me with smiling,
   After I've been long away.
Let us leave the slopes of " Low-wood,"
   Whence the " Langdale Pikes" seem near;
And behind us leaving " Doves' nest;"
   Let us skim o'er Windermere.

See how daylight is reclining
   On the lake in sweet repose,
As I often on thy bosom
   Rest my head, and gently doze.

And as thy long waving tresses
　　Hung above my sleeping brow ;
So the golden clouds of sunset
　　Gather o'er the mountains now.

In the tree-shade let us linger,
　　While we rest the dripping oar,
And we'll listen to the lipping
　　Of the water on the shore.
Sounds it not like lovers kissing,
　　Ere they part, and say adieu ;
Hear thee how it seems to linger,
　　And return, as lovers do.

Annie, in the silent evening,
　　When the breezes whisper low,
Love, methinks, becomes more tender,
　　For the heart seems all aglow.
Art thou not more glad to see me
　　In the peaceful vesper hour ?

When the thrush is singing sweetly,
   Near its own mate, in the bower?

ANNIE.

Sweetheart! I am ever joyful
   In thy presence, night or day;
But my heart knows fullest rapture
   In the evenings, golden-gray;
And upon the placid bosom
   Of the lake, we rest the oar;
And are listening to the lipping
   Of the water on the shore.

CHRISTMAS.

WELCOME! welcome! Christmas, welcome!
    To our homes once more;
Autumn, with her brow half-shaded,
And her auburn hair unbraided,
Faded cheeks, and garments faded,
    Died on Winter's shore.

Then the cold wind in compassion,
    Wove a shroud of snow;
Cover'd her in rough, kind fashion,
Moan'd a dismal lamentation,
Gush'd and sigh'd in desolation,
    A requiem of woe.

And he look'd around, and sorrow'd
    That the flowers were gone;
Swore if aught was still surviving,
That it should be ever-living,
Life from even snow receiving,
    That it should live on.

When he spied the brave old laurel,
    And the holly too,
And the mistletoe, just dying;
So he made them death-defying,
Not on summer sun relying,
    But to live years through.

Now they stay, like parting love looks,
    That won't take the wing,
Or like cherish'd hopes that linger
Pointing with a prophet's finger
To the sleeping crocus bringer,
    To the fresh young Spring.

But we use them now to cheer us,
    When we need most cheer;
When the nipping frosts are near us
And the robins do not fear us,
When old Christmas does endear us
    To the dying year.

Christmas, not with careworn furrows,
    Nor a bloodshot eye,
But an old age full of beauty,
Rich and mellow, ripe and fruity,
Last hour in a day of duty,
    Evening's western sky.

Christmas crown'd with red-eyed holly,
    And the mistletoe,
Deck'd with laurel, stooping lowly,
Smiling with a smile so holy,
Smiling on our young hearts' folly,
    Smiles with age should go.

Christmas, youth and age combining,
    Smiling on us all:
Christmas, winter's "silver-lining,"
Christmas, like a halo shining,
On the sad old years declining,
    On December's fall.

Welcome! with a three-fold welcome!
    Though thy head is bare,
Though the frost has tightly bound thee,
Though the snow may fall around thee,
Cold at heart we never found thee,
    Never frozen there.

Little children love to meet thee,
    Wast thou e'er a child?
Was the earth of thee deliver'd
When the little snow-drop quiver'd,
When the timid sunshine shiver'd,
    While the crocus smiled?

Yes! as gentle cold displacer,
    Life thou didst begin;
Now, the winter comes behind thee,
Welds the icy chains to bind thee,
But though feeble he may find thee,
    Thou hast spring within.

MAN AND MONKEY.

THERE are some despise the doctrine,
    That the monkeys bred the men,
But if monkeys came of sky-larks,
    All is surely right again.

We have everything within us,
    Birds and beasts and fishes, too,
Flowers and trees and rocks and metals,
    All the old and all the new.

Very microcosms are we,
    Just the world reduced in size ;

Seeds of earth to be transplanted
    To a land beyond the skies.

Man has come of all below him,
    All has been that *he might be*,
Earth is not alone his *mansion*,
    He's the world's *epitome*.

I can't prove that man *was* monkey,
    But assert thus much I can,
That whatever man has sprung from,
    There is monkey *now* in man.

And I think thus much is certain,
    And the truth we ought to know,
That unless a man is watchful,
    Into monkey he may go.

Then there comes the weighty question,
    Can we change to what *we're not*,

Thus, if man should prove a donkey,
   Where the donkey has he got?

Surely transmutation is not
   But degeneracy, shown,
So that man instead of rising,
   To his *lower self* has gone.

I have seen some human monkeys,
   And some donkeys I have seen,
And methinks that what man *may be*,
   Points to what he may *have been*.

Yet the question as to whether
   Man was monkey in the past,
Matters little, if we're growing
   Into angels at the last.

THE BLIGHTED FLOWER.

SUGGESTED BY THE DEATH OF A YOUNG LADY.

OH, it was sad in the bright young spring,
    When the sunbeams nourish the early bloom,
  The reaper Death, with his well-worn scythe,
    Cut down a flower, and unlock'd a tomb;
      'Twas a sorry deed, was that work of Death,
In the bright young spring, when the sweet birds sing.

  The tall trees look'd on the blighted bloom,
    And bow'd in the presence of hope's decay;
      The sweet birds above ceased their songs of love

They look'd on the dead and then flew away;
    And the soft breeze sigh'd through the weeping
        grove,
While the young spring shudder'd to see the tomb.

But an angel stood by the silent dead,
    And folded a jewel within her breast;
        'Twas the spirit-flower, which she would embower,
    In the heavenly garden, the home of rest:
        On the earth it lived for a single hour,
And would never die—so the angel said.

Then away they went, but not far away,
    To the land of an everlasting spring;
        And the flower so fair was planted there,
    Where the birds of Paradise ever sing,
        At peace in the heavenly Father's care,
Whose smile is the joy of unending day.

OH, WHAT YET UNOPEN'D CHAMBERS.

OH, what yet unopen'd chambers
   May there be within the soul,
That the future shall develope,
   As the silent ages roll.

Here we only enter being,
   Burst the shell and pierce the ground,
With but time to look and wonder,
   At the thousand things around.

Embryos we are of something
   That is greater than we know;

What we *are*, from what we *have been*,
    Shows the power of man to grow.

And unless the untried future,
    Stops the growth or fells the tree,
All the greatness left behind us
    Is as nought to what *shall be*.

Every hour we *live* is *harvest*,
    With the fruit of wisdom rife;
Every hour we *meet* is *pregnant*,
    Waiting for us with its life.

Not a failure is creation,
    But an all-fulfilling plan,
And the most unlike a failure,
    Is God's greatest creature man.

Deep within and all around him,
    There are wonders yet untold;

Every atom is a mountain,
    And the mountains bear the gold.

Every moment of existence
    Is a hieroglyphic scroll,
Full of meaning, rich in beauty,
    In the temple of the soul.

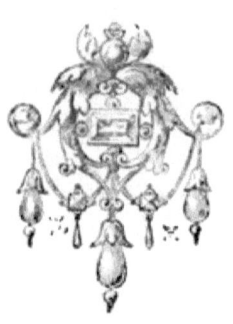

ENCOURAGEMENT.

Down in a cellar drunk
 A soul and body lay,
God's image marr'd and shrunk,
 And passing away.

Oh, 'twas a sight so sad
 To see that being there,
Who such a mission had
 To live and to declare :

Sinking beneath the beast,
 Wallowing deep in mire,

Acting the devil's priest,
    And kindling hell's own fire.

Wherefore, immortal one !
    Wherefore thy choice so low ?
Say is thy birthright gone,
    Thy right to choose and do ?

Art thou a man at all ?
    Did God on thee bestow
The power to choose and do—
    The choice of weal or woe ?

Is there within thy breast
    One remnant left of love ?
Or hast thou lull'd to rest
    By poison, that sweet dove ?

Surely thou art a man ;
    Or, if thou art not one,

Thou hast misshaped God's plan
  By folly of thine own.

But if thou 'rt man, why, then,
  Thou art my brother too;
And all things that I can
  I needs must for thee do.

The nearer death thou art,
  The more I 'm bound to strive
To keep thy better part
  By fanning it, alive.

I would not pass thee by,
  So wounded and so sore,
But take thee home and try
  Thy spirit to restore.

I know thou 'rt very weak,
  And that thy foes are strong:

But stirring words I'd speak
 To help thy heart along.

Thy weakness is thine own,
 Thou knowest that full well;
Thine enemies have grown
 By strength that from thee fell.

But do not lose thy heart,
 There's help for all who try;
And if thou dost thy part,
 Thy strength will live—not die.

JUSTICE

OUR God is just, and will have right,
    He doth demand it with His might.
'Tis true, but did you ever prove
How right it is to bless and love?
We must, indeed, the law obey;
But what's the law? doth Wisdom say.
"To bless and curse not," and to be
With all mankind in charity.
But then, methinks, I hear you say,
God need not, though man must obey:
He is above the law He made,
And if you bind Him you degrade.

I hear you, but I do not see
How He a King can truly be,
Who shows not in the highest sense
Himself the law's omnipotence.
God is the law, and did He say,
"Bless those who curse you" day by day?
And shall He curse the curser then—
And that with everlasting pain—
Returning evil with the same,
For ending sin, unending flame?
Nay, do not fear; He will not break
The law that He has deign'd to make:
But having said that we must "bless
Our enemies," He won't do less;
Nay more, for He'll increase our power
To take more blessing hour by hour.
To bless is ever right and just,
And bless and pardon all we must.
But if the "pound of flesh" we claim,
We ask for justice but in name.

MUSIC AND COLOURS.

OH, could we see the sounds we hear,
    Behold the music swell and rise,
What splendid colours would appear,
    What blending of the richest dyes!

The golden sunset in the west,
    The summer eve beyond the sea;
The sunrise from the Alpine crest,
    The high-noon sky from clouds all free;

The moonlight in the autumn-tide
    Shining upon the golden corn,
While clearest pearl-clouds softly glide
    And kiss the night till wakes the morn;

The glories of the summer clime,
    With breath-of-sapphire atmosphere,
Whose gorgeous beauties cheat old Time,
    And keep fair summer all the year ;—

Not these, nor thousand beauties more,
    Could for a moment equal be
To those full splendours that would pour
    Upon the spirit's ravish'd eye,

If Handel's " Hallelujah " strains
    In all their glories we could *see*,
Or if were cast athwart the plains
    Green of the " pastoral symphony ;"

Or if those mellow tune-full songs
    That need no words to tell their tale,
Arose like perfumed golden clouds,
    And floated on the sun-warm'd gale.

THE WIDOWER.

OH, leave me alone and be silent,
    Ay, leave me alone to-night;
I'd dwell in the past for a season,
    And muse by the red fire-light.

I'd sit with my feet on the fender,
    Near that untenanted chair,
And feel of *her* love till it seemeth
    That *she* once again sits there.

It's a year since the dear one left me,
    A year since it is to-day,

And the clouds that then gather'd round me,
    Still pall-like about me stay.

I knew that her days must be number'd,
    Knew by the flush on her cheek;
It was only the gilding of sunset,
    A departing glory streak.

I loved her a year as a maiden,
    A year I call'd her my wife,
And a year I've lived as an exile
    From all that is dear in life.

But she left me smiling so sweetly,
    As if she were turning round,
To tell me she look'd on the morning,
    And stood on celestial ground.

Then leave me alone and be silent,
    Ay, leave me alone to-night;

The Widower.

I'd sit with my feet on the fender,
    And muse by the red fire-light.

The Book of her choice still lies open,
    And there, at her fav'rite page;
How she loved the quaint, gentle Herbert!—
    She call'd him the sainted sage.

She ask'd me to read her the "Sunday,"
    The day that she took her flight,
And said she had oft spent with Herbert,
    That sweet day "most calm, most bright."

Since then I have not touch'd the volume,
    But think me to-night I may
And read through the beautiful "Temple,"
    So bright with the light of day.

Nay, I cannot, my hand would falter,
    Her spirit surrounds it yet,

The past seems as near as the present;
   Her reading I can't forget.

That Book must keep solemnly looking,
   Like sorrow for hope, in vain,
Till my heart like a daisy shall open,
   When morning returns again.

But I hear the knell and the tolling,
   I still see the mournful bier,
I still hear the funeral service,
   And still feel the scalding tear.

O God! how that "ashes to ashes"
   Pierced through me, an icy dart,
And the mould, as it fell on the coffin,
   Fell heavier on my heart.

I hear it as plainly as ever,
   An echoless, deathly tread,

That stamp'd on my hopes and my pleasures,
    And number'd them with the dead.

I'm a desolate wounded swallow,
    Left by its fellows alone;
While they, with the sunshine and summer,
    Away to new homes are gone.

I'm a poor broken-wingèd skylark,
    That flutters, but cannot fly,
Yet looks at the beautiful heavens,
    With yearning and tearful eye.

I long in my spirit for something
    That seemeth for ever gone;
Like swallow and lark I am wounded,
    And like them am sad and lone.

Then leave me alone in calm silence,
    Ay, leave me in peace to-night;
This *may* prove the hour of deep darkness,
    That borders the morning light.

PRAISE NOT OTHER LANDS TO ME.

THE Switzer boasts his mountains grand,
   That soar to reach the sky,
And bathe their feet in placid lakes,
   Where beauties, resting, lie.
Italia glories in her clime,
   That nurtures love and song,
Her vine-clad hills and floral vales,
   And her melodious tongue.
      But praise not other lands to me,
         Nor bid me through them roam;
      As fair as England they may be,
         But England is my home.

The German boasts of Fatherland,
 And loves it dearly too ;
And well he may, for England's Queen
 Proved German love was true.
Fair France can boast of her romance,
 Her Paris and her sky ;
While Spain against the world can show
 Her splendid woman's eye.
  But praise not other lands to me, &c.

O England! hallow'd shrine of home,
 And temple of the free,
The sacred Isle, where honour dwells
 With love and chivalry !
The metals found within thy hills
 Won't weld to chain for slave ;
While not a spot of ground but scorns
 To be a tyrant's grave.
  Then praise not other lands to me, &c.

The Fates may take me far away,
    And lead me o'er the sea,
But neither time nor change can win
    My English love from me:
No! never can I cease to feel
    The love old England gave—
'Tis stronger than the power of death,
    And triumphs o'er the grave.
    Then praise not other lands to me,
        Nor bid me through them roam;
    For England shall remember'd be
        When Heaven itself is home.

I AM SAD.

THE summer-time is full of flowers,
  The gardens all are gay;
They breathe the sunshine, drink the showers,
  And laugh the hours away.
The trees are clad in robes of green,
  And birds among them sing;
But I am sad, and can't be glad—
  My joy has ta'en the wing.

The brooks and rivers run along
  With music for the sea;

I am Sad.

The willows kiss them for the song,
   The breezes join the glee.
The joyous birds together play,
   Or chase each other on;
But I am sad, and can't be glad—
   My happy days are gone.

I used to love the summer-time,
   I used to love the spring;
But since my love has proved untrue,
   No joy to me they bring.
It seems as if the winter-time
   Had crept o'er all the year;
It's very cold within my heart—
   It's very dark and drear.

O heart of mine, with blighted love,
   What power thy life can save!
I'm like a yew-tree waiting death
   Beside an open grave:

The world itself seems but a tomb
   In which my love doth lie ;—
False-hearted man, I chide thee not,
   But loveless I must die.

ON A LATE SPRING.

OH, how I long for the Spring,—sweet Spring:
    I'm weary of Winter, weary of cold;
I'm waiting to hear the sweet birds sing,
    And I'm longing to see buds unfold.

The Spring-time is here, but the snow still falls,
    And the east wind bitterly, fiercely blows,
The icicles hang on the garden walls,
    And the bare trees shrink as from coming foes.

And my feet are tired of the frozen ground,
    I'm weary of seeing my steaming breath;
The crisp is no longer a welcome sound,
    But comes like an echo of lingering death.

On a Late Spring.

Oh, my heart is wearying day by day
   To walk by the brooks while the sweet birds sing :
No cattle can long for the grassy May
   As I for the sunshine and joy of Spring.

The snow-drops and crocusses have been sent,
   As the fond dove was from the ark of old ;
But without the hedge-budding fair portent,
   They needs must return if it keeps so cold.

Yet the light is lengthening a span a day,
   And morning and evening each takes a share ;
And the light comes of heat, the wise ones say,
   And if that be so, I need have no care.

I 'm a little impatient—want more faith,
   For the Spring will come spite of frost or gale ;
I 'm apt to forget what the Scripture saith,
   That "seed-time and harvest shall never fail."

MARRIAGE.

WHEN mortals marry,—angels sing
    Their sweetest, richest, choral strains,
And ever to the altar bring
    Flowerets from the heavenly plains,
        And they bedeck the bridal pair
        With something more than common care.

But why are angels fill'd with joy,
    At these heart unions here below?
And why should they their harps employ,
    And strike them with such fervour too?
        Ah! why indeed, if not to prove
        That Heaven itself is naught but love!

TH' SEXTON TO HIS SPADE.

DIG away, dig! goo on owd spade,
  Death has been at it again ;
He keeps up a regular trade,
  Slaughterin' childer o' men :
    Owd folk an' young,
    Weak folk and strong,
  All ha' to follow whatever they sen.

Give 'em their six foot long by two,
  Measure it honest and fair ;
Give 'em to every inch 'ut's due,
  Ay, dig 'em their gradely share.
    High folk an' low,
    Down they mun go,
  Let 'em ha' plenty, an' summut to spare.

Th' Sexton to his Spade.

Dig away, dig! through sand an' clay!
   Think as yo 're makin' a bed,
An' somebody in 't 'ull ha' to lay
   Wi' never a blanket spread.
      Smooth it your best,
      Bones may want rest,
Achin' mayn't a' be gone eawt when they 're dead.

Worms are waitin', they seem to know
   Both me an' my busy spade ;
Churchyard worms are fattest of o',
   They 're plump, like a lady's maid ;
      Aw 've seen 'em peep
      Down th' grave so deep
As if they wonder'd if th' coffin 'd be lead.

Aw 've sometoimes thowt as they sent a spy
   To watch where aw broke a sod,
They look so fo'se when aw 've pass'd 'em by,
   An' gan me a sort o' nod ;

>   An' then they 'd run,
>   As women dun
> When they 'n getten news, to scatter abroad.

Dig away, dig! my turn 'ull come-
  A sexton, loike th' rest, mun dee ;
He sees a lot o' folk taen whoam,
  An' then in his turn goes he :
    But me an' th' spade
    'Ull stick to th' trade
  Till somebody has t' dig a grave for me.

Earth goes to earth ; and dust to dust
  We all mun return, they say ;
We conna buy an hour on trust.
  But death 's a bill we mun pay :
    Th' yammerin' grave
    Its share 'ull have,
  It 's no use ossin' t' be runnin' away.

THE OLD YEAR TO A LITTLE GIRL.

I 'VE just come to say "good-bye" to you, Millie
I 've just come to say " good-bye ;"
    I 'm the present year,
    And am not long here,
So I 've just come to say "good-bye."

I shall soon be away from all time, Millie—
I shall soon be away from all time ;
    I 'm going to the past,
    To the year that was last,
To the years that have been in all time.

But I 'm not going away to die, Millie—
No, I 'm not going away to die;
    In the deeds that are done,
    I still shall live on,
For good deeds or bad cannot die.

But I shall see you again e'er long, Millie—
I shall see you again before long;
    And you 'll know me quite well
    By the tales I shall tell—
Yes! I shall see you again before long.

So I 've just come to say " good-bye " to you, Millie—
Yes, I 've just come to say " good-bye;"
    And I hope, my sweet dear,
    That in the next year
To be better than ever you 'll try.

FLOWERS.

FLOWERS are more than simple beauties
   To *adorn* this world of ours;
There is something human in them—
   We have kinship with the flowers.

When we see the lovely roses,
   And we love them passing well,
It is from some other roses
   That within our bosom's dwell.

There is not a single floweret,
   Blade of grass, or bird, or tree,

Flowers.

That in essence and perfection
   Is not ever more in me.

And as birds oft pipe, and others
   Answer to the loving call ;
So the beauties of creation
   Speak their fellows in us all.

Love brings summer to the spirit,
   And awakes the birds to song—
Fills the soul with life and beauty,
   Till in very joy they throng.

Then it is the birds within us
   Pipe to others all around,
And the flowers and trees in nature
   Smile to hear the *double sound*.

TO LITTLE "WILLIE."

I WONDER where thy brother is,
      Sweet little " Will."
God sent thee just in time on earth
      His place to fill.

I used to love thy brother well,
      And he loved me;
And many happy hours he's sat
      Upon my knee.

And oft he stood and pulled my beard,
      Brave little boy;
And when I started as if hurt,
      He laughed for joy.

To Little "Willie."

I loved thy brother since he was
           A few days old;
And oh! I loved him till he turned
           So pale and cold.

Thou wast but three days old when he
           Slipped out of sight,
As if he had some corner turned,
           So swift his flight.

He was full well as yesterday,
           And dead to-day—
His life had not been lighted long,
           Ere snuffed away.

I saw him to thy mother brought,
           Close to her bed—
And thou wast in the room as well
           While he lay dead.

Oh! "Willie," it was very sad
    To see that sight.
The pale moon looking on a flower,
    Killed by a blight.

Thy mother fondled o'er his form,
    And stroked his cheek:
And though she knew he could not hear,
    She still would speak.

His eye was closed, his mouth was still,
    So stiff he lay;
But oh! his mother could not think
    The form was clay.

She took his little hand in hers,
    And then his feet,
And then she smoothed his flaxen hair
    So straight and neat.

To Little "Willie."

Her hand was just as fair as his,
   But not so pale :
How slight the change from life to death.
   How thin Death's veil !

But he had gone, and as he went
   To heaven above,
It seemed as if my heart went too,
   Drawn by his love.

How beautiful it is to think
   That he is there,
More lovely than he was on earth,
   More pure, more fair.

I'm sure he is an angel now.
   In heaven's bright home,
Awaiting all his earthly friends
   When they shall come.

And "Willie," when I go to heaven,
    I hope that he
Will make me welcome as on earth
    I used to be.

And as I took him by the hand,
    When he was here,
I hope that he will show me heaven
    When I get there.

He will have learned what I must learn,
    And, oh, what joy,
He'll walk me through the Angel Homes,
    An Angel Boy!

Oh, "Willie," bless thy bright-blue eyes
    And happy face;
Come now and nestle in my heart,
    Near Charlie's place.

And come and sit where Charlie did
>On my right knee,
And with thy little untaught tongue
>Speak love to me.

Or "Willie," let us hand in hand
>Together go,
And walk among the garden beds
>Where posies grow.

For thou art just a little flower,
>And I a tree;
And if the wind should coldly blow,
>I'll shelter thee.

I'll love thee for thy brother's sake,
>And for thine own;
Thank God for two such tender loves
>In one heart sown.

SONNET.

(Written on finding that Abraham Lincoln had been elected President, on the platform that the Constitution shall be amended so as to render Slavery for ever illegal.)

AWAKE! ten thousand times ten thousand lyres,
Awake! rejoice! be jubilant, and fill
The universe with your immortal strains!
Give song a very day of revelry!
Let every instrument that can express
A heart's deep joy answer the call, and swell
The music of expanding harmonies
That rise to Heaven, and meet rejoicing there!

Let all that makes up glorious harmony
Join with the myriad voices that now raise
Loud songs of gladness to the throne of God,
A nation has repented of her sin!
The right has conquered in her strife with wrong!
The chains fall crumbled, and the slaves go free!

MORNING HYMN.

GREAT God, Thou giver of my days,
   Assist my heart to give Thee praise,
A morning hymn I'd sing to Thee,
Oh, may it, Lord, accepted be.

The morn has chased the night away,
Darkness has fled before the day ;
Ten thousand birds their matins sing,
Till praise itself seems on the wing.

The hills and valleys, woods and streams,
Are glad beneath Sol's golden beams,
And from a myriad altars rise
The incense of Earth's sacrifice.

Morning Hymn.

And I with grateful heart would raise
To Thee my morning hymn of praise,
And dedicate afresh to Thee
The powers which Thou hast given me.

Oh, be Thou, Lord, my morning light,
Arise in me and chase the night,
Be Thou my sun while here I stay,
And light me on to brighter day.

PRAISE.

FOR all the flowers that bloom and smile
   In happy summer days,
In life to cheer, in death to cure,
   Good Lord, I give Thee praise.

For birds that sing, and bees that hum,
   For streams that musing flow,
For all sweet sounds that tune my heart
   The pure and good to know.

For breezes, that are perfumed sighs
   From nature's loving breast;

For hurricanes, that clear the air
   Of what would else infest.

For Thy right hand and stretch'd-out arm,
   Which moulds, but never mars:
For darkness, that reveals the light—
   For night, that shows the stars.

For earth, that is not merely dust,
   But mother of the flowers;
For clouds, that sail like ships in air
   With cargoes of rich showers.

For love of children, and their love
   So pure and undefiled;
For this, that though I'm now a man,
   To feel I've been a child.

For every throb of human love,
   For proof that man is true;

For heroes who in humble life,
    Unheard of, strive and do.

For true humility, which grafts
    On life's dark sad yew-tree ;
For pain and sorrow, that awake
    True sympathy in me.

For all experiences in life,
    For sunshine and for shade ;
For good that is, and ill that seems,
    Of which our lives are made.

For prophets, who have told the truth,
    And pointed out Thy ways ;
For science, one of Thy "high priests,"
    That loudly sings Thy praise.

For disappointment's icy grasp,
    That stops the running fool ;

For loss and cross, that send us back
   Like truants to the school.

For humble hope and lofty faith,
   And love that is divine,
For "hands cut off" and "eyes pluck'd out,"
   When they too much were mine.

For all Thy loving providence,
   That shapeth out our ways;
For blessings in ten thousand forms,
   Good Lord, I give thee praise!

"IF I MAKE MY BED IN HELL, BEHOLD, THOU ART THERE."

WHY there, Thy presence Lord, why there?
    In those dark, dismal realms below;
Shall devils in thy goodness share?
    Shall devils of thy mercy know?

Th' inhabitants of that dark place
    Forsook Thee of their own free will;
They spurn'd the offers of Thy grace,
    And chose the path that led to ill.

The doom of every one is just;
    Each condemnation is its own,

If I make my Bed in Hell,

And every soul acknowledge must,
    That good and right have both been shown.

For none can look to Thee, O God!
    And blame Thee for the pain they bear;
For never dost Thou use a rod
    That parent love could hold or spare.

But what Thy mission, Lord, in hell?
    What takes Thee to that dark abode?
Could angel bands not do as well,
    And spare the dignity of God?

Oh, foolish thought, and question too:
    God's love's a sea without a coast,
A limitation never knew;
    But most is seen where needed most.

What need of mercy, if no wrong?
    What need forgiveness, if no sin?

What means compassion, deep and strong,
   If all are happy, pure, and clean?

Shall pain that's almost infinite
   And feeding ever on despair,
Be reigning with a god-like might,
   And Love and Mercy not be there?

Nay! God is merciful to all,
   And full of love to those who need;
He helpeth up the lame who fall,
   And bindeth up the wounds that bleed.

No case so bad, but His great heart
   Still yearns to comfort and to bless;
The good Samaritan's His part,
   Man would be this—God can't be less.

On Earth—in Hell—below—above,
   No place or state can lack His care:

No distance can from Him remove,
    For God and love are everywhere.

There's not in all the universe
    A corner where He is not found;
And never does He take a curse,
    But strews thick blessings o'er the ground.

And shall we say that those whose sin
    Has sunk them to the dark abyss,
Are past the power of love to win
    Again to purity and bliss?

That God who gave us life at first,
    Can't perfect us by all His skill,
Nor make the best without the worst,
    But finds He's conquer'd by free-will.

Did e'er He make a power so strong
    That e'en His own it could defy?

Or aught that could become so wrong,
   As to be wrong eternally?

I would not dare to underrate
   The gift of God that makes us men;
Nor aught of truth to understate,
   However stern or fraught with pain.

But this I say, and feel it true,
   That man has naught which God the King
Can't with it as He chooses do,
   And will not to perfection bring.

His modes of action are His own;
   Nor does He all His meaning tell;
But surely this much can be shown,
   That if there be a place called Hell,

It is in purpose and design
   A very furnace for the soul,

If I make my Bed in Hell,

Where all the dross we must resign,
   To have it pure, and clean, and whole.

For He who made us all of gold,
   Or silver, as His will might be,
Will rid us of alloy, and mould
   Us to His perfect imagery.

I don't presume to understand
   How God controls a will that's free ;
It is His master-work—too grand
   For mortal vision e'er to see.

I'm thankful that He gave me breath,
   And with it this assurance, too,
That life can never end in death—
   For death's the gate it rises through.

I will not ask too much to-day,
   But patiently await the hour

When He shall take my soul away
  To clearer truth and greater power.

And there I'll study face to face
  The truths now hidden half from veiw,
And will ten thousand wonders trace
  Up to their source in God the true.

And often will I turn my gaze
  Back to my earth life, that I may
See there the wonders of God's ways,
  Leading through darkness up to day.

Yea, Hell itself I'll gaze upon,
  And see my Maker's doings there,
Changing the curse and weary groan
  To humble penitence and prayer.

And as eternal ages roll,—
  Ages too long by years to tell,
I shall behold a perfect whole,
  Without a sin, or pain, or Hell.

MARRIAGES AND DEATHS.

ON such a day, at such a place,
    By such a one, 'tis said,
A loving pair resolved to share
    One home—one loaf of bread.

But prithee go a line below,
    And read you what is said :
A loving pair is severed there,—
    For death with one has fled.

If parting comes so certain then,
    Is't wise on earth to wed,

If ever after meeting smiles,
    The parting tears are shed?

Let those who are bereavèd speak,
    And hear you what is said:
Though 'twere, indeed, but for a week,
    We surely would be wed.

For though we part, we meet again,
    And ever after tread
In perfect oneness, yonder plains
    Where all our hopes have fled.

For Marriage is a gift of worth,
    The best that God hath given;
But should be planted first on earth,
    Then perfected in heaven.

GRIEF.

WHEREFORE the power so wonderful in man
    To wear alike the garb of bliss or woe?
To feel the rapture of a new-born love,
Or bear the stinging of a poisoned grief?
To bask in all the sunshine of a hope,
Or shrink beneath the thunders of despair?
Why were the nerves so tempered, that sweet sounds
And harsh discordances could play thereon?
Oh, cold philosophy, thy moonlight rays
Can bring no summer to my ice-bound soul,
Thy shrill night blast can make no morn for me,
Thy glow-worm light is but a mocking show.

Grief.

Did we not walk together, he my friend,
And I, for five-and-twenty years and more ?
Did not our friendship weave like warp and woof
To make one piece, and not a thread was lost ?
Did not the " gentleness" that " made him great"
Melt all his passion into sweet perfume ?
So that indignant and immensely strong,
He yet was kindly to his very foes,
And brought them weeping to his feet at last ?
Did he not labour for the common good,
And strive with words of iron truth and power,
All molten into fervid eloquence,
To prove the right, and triumph o'er the wrong ?
And shall not future ages wreath his name
With flowers of praises from the poor man's
    heart,
To gaze in wonder on so fair a fame ?

So wise in counsel, and withal so just,
Truth unrefracted by a selfish aim ;

Such tenderness and strength combined, that he
A Cupid was and Hercules in one.

This was my friend, all this ; but how much more
It needs not me to tell, for all earth knows ;
And Heaven ere this has claimed him as its own,
While God the King has bid him, "Come up high."

LINES ON RETURNING A POCKET-HANDKERCHIEF TO A LADY.

AND can I really let thee go—
　Can I from thee ever part?
A thousand voices answer No!
　Thou art the kerchief of my heart.

How often have I on thee looked
　With silent, long, and earnest gaze!
And, oh, what sonnets have I booked,
　Each letter written in thy praise!

I've thought about thee day by day,
　I've slept upon thee through the night;

And, oh, the tears thou 'st wiped away—
    Why, they would be *a notion* quite.

But who can all thy virtues tell,
    Who shall count thy duties done?
Duties that are known full well
    Known, indeed, to "Annie" one.

Yes, who could ever hope to sing,
    Aught like worthily of thee;
Or an offering hope to bring,
    That acceptable would be?

Is there any perfume known—
    "Jockey Club," or "Kiss me quick,"
"Lavender," or "*Eau de Cologne*,"
    "Pachoulay," or "Pretty Dick;"

That would not offensive be
    To thyself so sweet and pure?

It's plain indeed as R. R. B.,
   That but the last thou couldst endure.

Yet we must part; too true, alas!
   The fates have willed it to be so;
And I, alone, my life must pass;
   Say! canst thou give me *such a blow!*

But all is lost, and I have done,
   And now must feed upon my woes:
I'll only ask that, when alone,
   Thou'lt think of my dear Roman nose.

I'll think of thee from day to day,
   And through the years as on they roll,
And all my tears shall flow away,
   For want of thee, *upon my sole.*

A VALENTINE.

THERE is a place they call Oak Brook,
   Where some folks *dye;*
And if I ain't so much mistook,
   Some folks sigh;
      So do I.

But *dying* is so great a treat,
   When Cupid slays,
That I would run that death to meet,
   A thousand ways,
      All my days.

A Valentine.

But, Cupid, why not throw your dart
    While I stay here?
And let it pierce right through my heart
    From Staffordshire;
        Yes, do dear.

But what if I'm obliged to say,
    I am death-struck;
And hope you're in the self-same way,
    A dying duck!
        Oh, what luck!

Why, then, I would this plan suggest,
    That thou shouldst be
The doctor to my bleeding breast,
    And I'll cure thee.
        Dost agree?

LINES TO A LADY, WITH THE AUTHOR'S "CARTE."

ENCLOSED you'll see my shadow *lies*,
    And though 'twere strange to tell,
And may your humble self surprise,
    It *speaks the truth* right well.

And though it is one-sided, still
    It is *impartial* too ;
For I have not a " *better half*,"
    Nor *worse* than that in view.

And if you put it in a *frame*,
    No matter what the kind,

Or call it by whatever name,
   'Twill prove a "frame of mind."

Yet if, while you are looking at
   My shadow made secure,
Your heart should beat like "*pit-a-pat*,
   Remember I'm the "*Cure.*"

And note, that though it may seem smart,
   It plainly can be shown,
That by my humble little "*carte*"
   My *carriage* may be known.

LINES TO A LADY WHO SENT HER "CARTE" TO THE AUTHOR.

As sure as I am " Pretty Dick,"
   As sure as you are " Lovely Nancy,"
The " Carte " you sent me on so quick,
   Both claims my thanks and suits my fancy.

I'll place it in an honour'd page,
   'Twill grace my album and adorn it ;
And oh ! I'll fly in such a rage,
   If any one should dare to scorn it.

I'll grow quite jealous, stamp, and swear
   The fellow is a vile Gorilla,

Lines to a Lady.

My handkerchief to bits I'll tear,
   Then sit and smoke a good " Manilla."

Or if you like I'll go quite mad;
   Or, like the fair " Ratcatcher's Daughter,"
I'll poison take, which would be sad;
   Or drown myself in dirty water.

But as I do not know the man
   Who will not say the " Carte " is splendid.
I think 'twill be a wiser plan
   To wait till life by time is ended.

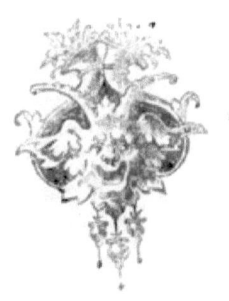

TINKLE, TINKLE, TINY BROOKLET.

TINKLE, tinkle, tiny brooklet,
    Tinkle ever on your way;
Cut the sunshine into diamonds,
Into pearl beads cut the moonlight:
    Dash them on your little spray;
    Gaily glisten night and day.

Tinkle, tinkle, tiny brooklet,
    Tinkle, tinkle, as you go;
Catch the music of the morning,
Catch the music of the noontide;
    Bear them with you as you flow,
    To the mellow evening glow.

Tinkle, Tinkle, Tiny Brooklet.

Tinkle, tinkle, tiny brooklet,
    Tinkle ever far and near,
Just as if the skylark warbling,
With the notes of all the singers,
    Fell into your bosom clear,
    There to live and re-appear.

Tinkle, tinkle, tiny brooklet,
    Sparkle in the summer sun,
At the bottom of the valley,
Like a baby in a cradle,
    Through your mossy borders run,
    Full of laughter, full of fun.

Tinkle, tinkle, tiny brooklet,
    Through the deep and wooded glen ;
Now beneath entwining branches,
Now below o'erhanging grasses ;
    Now quite hid, now seen again,
    Keep on tinkling through the glen.

Tinkle, tinkle, tiny brooklet,
    Tinkle, tinkle to the trees,
Let the fern leaves, bending, listen;
Let the wild flowers drink the music;
    Let the moonlit summer breeze
    Bear your sweet love melodies.

Tinkle, tinkle, my life's brooklet,
    On your ever-winding way,
Through the dell, or through the meadow,
Under rocks or over pebbles—
    Still go tinkling night and day;
    Music ceases if you stay.

TO MY MOTHER,

ON HER SEVENTY-FIRST BIRTHDAY.

MOTHER, I've gather'd from my heart
   Some flowers and leaves all bright and gay
And I have made of them a wreath
   To place around thy brow to-day.
The years have mounted up so high,
   They've touch'd thy hair and made it gray;
But I would crown the years and thee
   With flowers that will not fade away.

The fires that kindled life at first
   And glow'd so brightly in thy breast,
Have burn'd so long, that all thy soul
   In blessing has become most blest:

And all thy nature so warm'd through,
   That now I deem thee at thy best :
Thy Eastern sky was bright and warm,
   But full of glory is thy West.

Mother, I do remember well,
   When I was but a little child,
How thou didst draw me to thy breast,
   And clasp me with a passion wild—
As if thou didst desire to merge
   Thy very nature in thy child—
While I did nestle near thy heart,
   And thought thy heaving bosom smiled.

I would not lose for all the world,
   That recollection of thy love,
But hold it as a jewel, set
   In tender memories, far above
The value of ten thousand gems
   Which Lapidaries could improve :

And I will take it when I die,
    And show it to the King above.

And, mother, when thy life below
    Is finish'd, and thy work is done,
As thou dost enter yonder world,
    Where life in deeper streams shall run
If they should ask thee at the gate
    What fame or honour thou hast won :
Tell them, and tell it proudly too,
    That thou wast lovèd by thy son.

THE MAN WHO IS KIND TO ANOTHER.

THIS world is so hard and so stony,
    That if a man is to get through,
He need have the courage of Nelson,
    And plenty of Job's patience too.
But a man who is kind to another,
    And cheerfully helps him along,
We'll claim as a man and a brother,
    And here's to his health in a song.

This life is as cheerless as winter
    To those who are cold in the heart,

But the man who is warm in his nature
  Bids winter for ever depart.
The ground that he treads on will blossom,
  Till beauties around him shall throng ;
God bless such a man and a brother,
  An here's to his health in a song.

As clouds that in sunshine are open,
  Are silver'd by light passing through,
So men who are generous in spirit,
  Are bless'd by the good deeds they do.
There's nothing like helping another
  For getting one's own self along ;
Who does this is truly a brother,
  And here's to his health in a song.

There's something in other men's sorrows
  That strengthens a man who is true,
They melt him at first, and then mould him,
  The manliest actions to do.

The Man who is Kind to Another.

There's lots of both sorrow and trouble,
Our poor fellow-creatures among;
But God makes the blessings all double
To those who help others along.

WELCOME TO GARIBALDI.

BRITANNIA, get thy helmet on,
   And go thou to the sea;
Caprera's master leaves his home
   And comes to visit thee.

Right royally receive thy guest,
   And give him hand for hand;
He is thy equal, and 'twere best
   On level ground to stand.

'Twere fitter thou shouldst go and meet
   This man with lofty brow,

Than that thy queenly face should greet
  All kings on earth, I trow.

For though no richly jewell'd crown
  Is seen his brow to shade,
He gave a kingdom, then bow'd down
  Before the king he'd made.

Go haste thee, then, Britannia, haste,
  And let him welcome be ;
For though he has not royal taste,
  Yet more than king is he.

No craven spirit does he bear,
  Nor sycophantic smile ;
The badge of manhood's all he'll wear,
  No other's worth his while.

He is a warrior and a brave,
  And in the wars has bled ;

Welcome to Garibaldi.

His home and fatherland to save,
    His precious blood was shed.

The people waited long and long,
    Till threaten'd with despair,
While earth's fair paradise of song
    Was wasted and laid bare.

Like strangers in a foreign land,
    Although at home were they,
While their oppressors did demand
    Of them a cheerful lay.

'Twas hard beneath the cloven hoof,
    The pleasant song to sing ;
'Twas hard beneath the prison roof,
    To give to joy the wing.

'Twas hard to bear oppression's rule,
    And feel the tyrant's rod ;

'Twas hard to learn in such a school,
    Pure faith in right and God.

The warrior heard the people's cry,
    And felt their load of wrong;
The patriot spirit was not dry,
    But weeping made him strong.

He moved himself to break the yoke
    His brethren long had worn,
And having thought to make the stroke,
    Resolve was quickly born.

His sword was driven in the ground,
    His face he raised on high,
One hand upon his sword he laid,
    And one was on his thigh.

And thus with forehead broad and bare,
    Before the Living God,

A solemn vow, and earnest prayer,
   Were register'd aloud.

Not arm of flesh could make him stay,
   Not power of earth could hold;
His people's chains he'd break away,
   Or slave himself be sold.

And it was done.   Italia rose
   Emancipated, free;
And yet not all, for still the foes
   Hold part in slavery.

But wait! for Garibaldi's heart
   Shall not to dust return,
Till Italy in every part
   To freedom shall be born.

And when at length the land is free,
   And he has pass'd from sight,

The guardian angel he shall be
  Of Italy, and right.

In England then, where Alfred reign'd
  The greatest king on earth,
We'll pay him homage all unfeign'd —
  The homage due to worth.

And not a nation 'neath the sun
  Shall give so grand a cheer,
As Liberty's incarnate son
  Shall have on coming here.

Go meet him then, Britannia, go,
  The fair should meet the brave;
And as he were thy brother, show
  The welcome he should have.

I'VE KNOWN THE RICH MAN DIE.

I'VE known the rich man die,
    The man of notes and gold ;
His latter end was misery,
    For peace had long been sold,—

Sold for the glittering earth,
    Sold for a paper roll ;
He'd barter'd eternal worth
    For trash, and spoil'd his soul.

Starved out his better man,
    Blotted God's image fair,
And shrivell'd and shrunk and wan,
    But a skeleton man was there.

His treasure had been on earth,
    And there his heart was still;
Pity to him was death—
    Love but a deathly chill.

All that he loved was gold;
    All that he wanted, fame;
His love had been cast in a mould
    Of earth, and received its name.

For himself in life he'd wrought,
    For others had no care,
And the needy in his thought
    Had neither place nor share.

And now on his bed he lies,
    Ending his mortal life,
Striving to hope and pray,
    But feeling how vain the strife.

Prayer is the good man's speech,
   'Tis not the cry of fear;
Love 'tis alone can reach
   To the celestial sphere.

Prayer is a grace that grows,
   Ripening hour by hour;
And who most prays best knows
   Of its amazing power.

Money that is not made
   The means of doing good,
Maketh a two-edged blade
   That draws the soul's best blood.

Think of it, you who live,
   Think of it while you may;
Money can never give
   Peace to the dying day.

I AM A LITTLE VALENTINE.

I AM a little Valentine,
    And came to bless mamma,
But now that she to heaven has gone,
    I'll love and cheer papa.

I am a little snowdrop fair,
    The harbinger of spring;
The cold departs when I appear,
    And birds begin to sing.

I am a little crocus too,
   Just peeping into day;
Pointing all the March winds through,
   To warm and merry May.

I am a little star of love,
   Twinkling as I shine;
And, as the stars, I'll constant prove,
   A welcome Valentine.

And as I tall and older grow,
   By this my natal day,
I'll try, like Valentines, to throw
   Some sunshine on life's way.